Eunice Kennedy Shriver

Inspiring Olympics for All

Jenna Grodzicki

Sports for All

Eunice Kennedy Shriver loved sports. She thought all kids could be fast and strong.

She thought everyone should have a chance to compete.

Jump into Fiction

A Day at the Beach

Eunice runs down the beach. "I'll race you!" she calls to her sister Rosemary.

The sisters love to go, go, go!
Eunice dives into the water.
She swims right through a big
wave.

“Let’s build a sand castle,”
Eunice says to Rosemary.
The sisters get out of the water
and start to dig.

They smile.
It is a great day.

Back to Nonfiction

Growing Up

Eunice came from a large family. She had eight brothers and sisters. The family spent a lot of time outside. In summer, they would swim and sail. In winter, they would ski and skate on the ice.

Middle Child

Eunice was born on July 10, 1921. She was the fifth child born in her family.

Eunice loved to play tennis.
She played a lot with her sister Rosemary.
Rosemary was disabled.
But that did not stop her.
She would hit the ball and play hard.

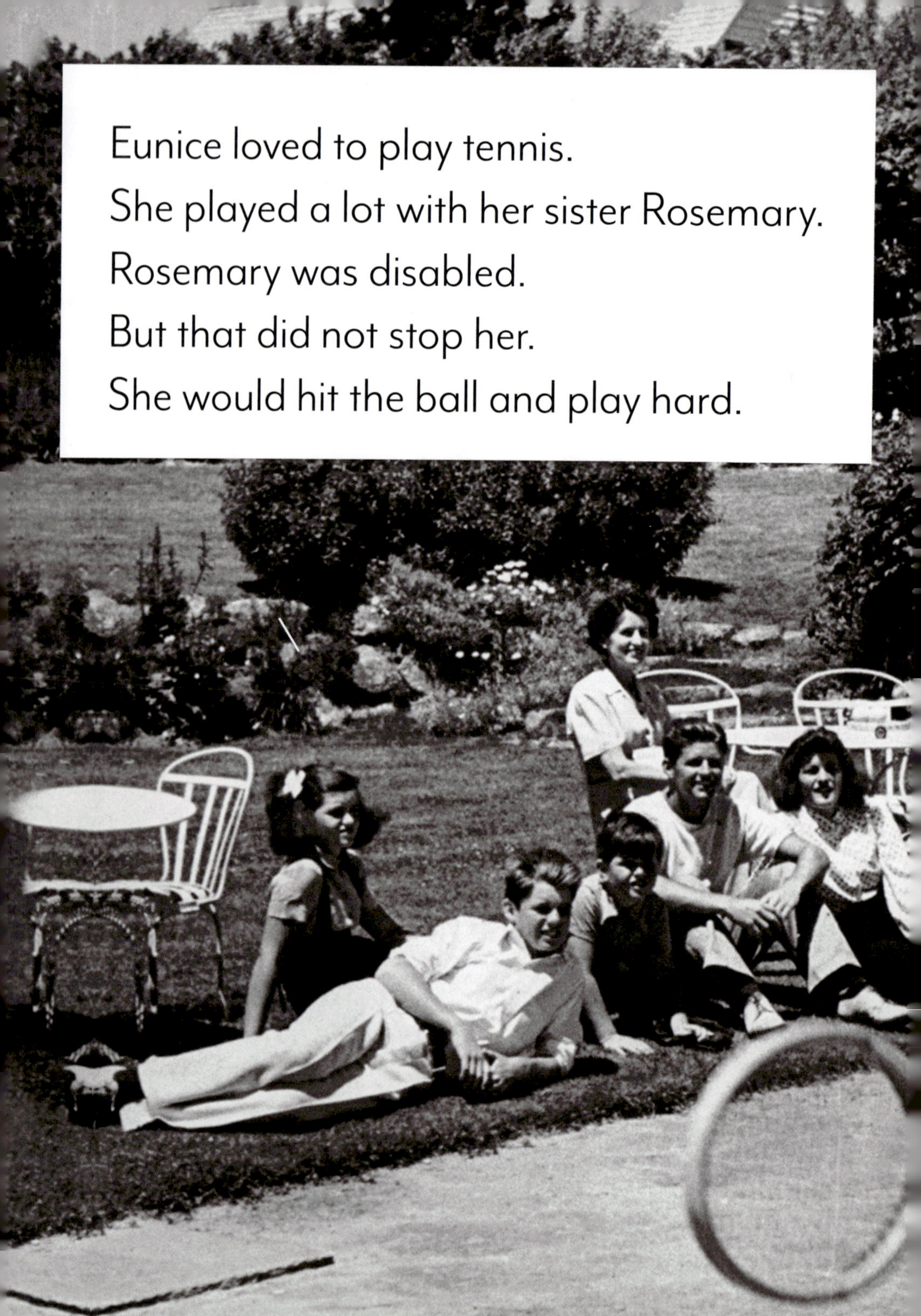

Eunice

Enough

When Eunice was young, people with disabilities could not join a gym.
They could not go to summer camp.
They had few chances to play sports.
Eunice thought that was unfair.
"Enough," she said.
So, she opened a special place for people with disabilities to play.

Name Change

In 1953, Eunice married R. Sargent Shriver Jr.
They had five children. She changed her name from Eunice Kennedy to Eunice Kennedy Shriver.

Think and Talk

What can you tell about the sisters from this photo?

Camp Shriver

Eunice set up a camp in her backyard.
She called it Camp Shriver.
More than 100 children with disabilities came to the camp.
They got to play sports and games.
They could swim and ride horses.
Camp Shriver was a big success!

Calling All Campers

Camp Shriver opened in 1962.
Eunice's children joined the camp too.
They played with the campers.

Camp Shriver was open four summers.
Older students helped at the camp.
They taught and coached the campers.
The camp grew bigger each year.
Many people came to watch the games.
They saw kids working hard.
They saw kids making friends.

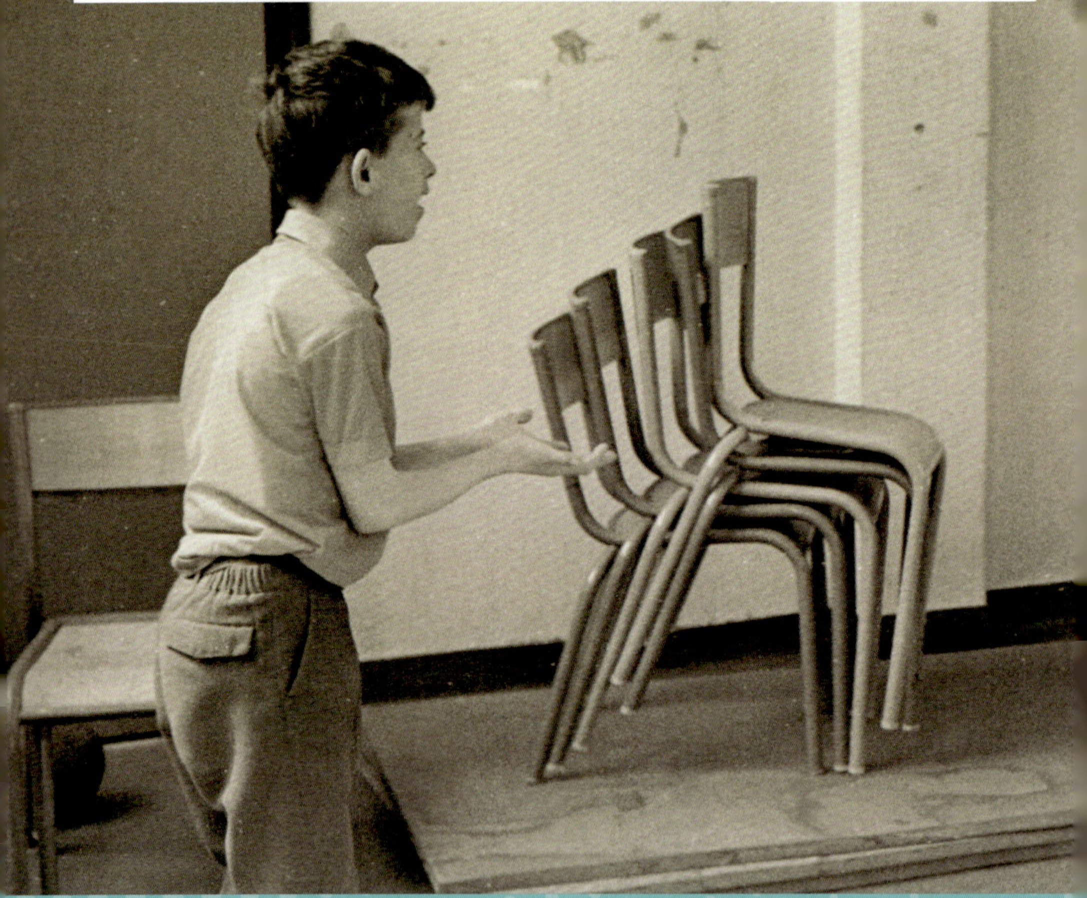

A New Plan

Eunice loved Camp Shriver.
But she hoped to do more.
She wanted all kids to have a chance to compete.
So, Eunice made a new plan.
She asked other people to help with her plan.
Her plan was to start the Special Olympics.

The Special Olympics

The first Special Olympics took place in Chicago, Illinois.

Athletes waved flags.

A man carried a torch.

The athletes made friends.

Some athletes won medals.

The mayor said, "The world will never be the same."

He was right.

A Big Success

The first event took place on July 20, 1968.

There were 1,000 athletes there.

They came from the United States and Canada.

SPECIAL OLYMPICS
MARYLAND

Today, more than five million athletes are part of each Special Olympics.
They come from all over the world.
Fans fill the stands to watch the events.
They clap and cheer loudly.
Eunice started something big.
She showed the world what athletes with disabilities can do.

Legacy

Eunice died on August 11, 2009. Her work still helps people.

Civics in Action

Eunice Kennedy Shriver wanted to include everyone. You can too. Make a buddy bench at school! It is a place kids can go when they do not have someone to play with.

1. Decide where your buddy bench will be.
2. Make a sign for the bench.
3. Explain to others in your class and school what the buddy bench is.
4. Include others in games when they sit on the buddy bench.